LOVE AND LOU

First of all, thank you for purchasing this book. We have worked hard to create a beautiful, custom experience that shows the greatness of my city. This is not your typical coloring or activity book. This book includes coloring pages, wordfinds, fact, recipes, and some of my favorite places in Louisville.

Have fun with this book. Enjoy yourself. Take time to explore this great city of Loisville and realize that this book is just a taste. Stay Connected, Follow us on Instagram @InFlyWeTrustInc, and Stay Fly.

If you like this,
PLEASE, PLEASE, PLEASE
leave a review and find more of our products at

www.InFlyWeTrust.com

-Jide Fresh

The "Love and Lou" Playlist can be found at this link.

Linktr.ee/inflywetrust

This coloring book is dedicated to the city that raised me. But for 21 years I loved this city from a distance. I returned recently and the homecoming I have received has been extremely humbling. Louisville has reignited a love for the city that birthed me and in my rebirth, I have become an artist in Louisville. Thank you, Louisville for being kind to me. Thank you, Louisville for encouraging me. Thank you, Louisville for being the peace I needed to transform into the person that I wanted to be. But there is one thing about this city that saddens me. It is that it is its own best-kept secret to the people here. People from other cities recognize the potential that is here. This could be an up north Atlanta or a down south Chicago. The artistry, nature, food, festivities, and more make this city what it is. But most important are the people. Louisville, love each other. Care for one another. And make Louisville Weird again! Also, I have not been endorsed by anyone or any place in this book.
These are just some of my favorite spots in the city.
Enjoy!

LOUISVILLE WAS ALSO A GOOD PLACE FOR BEING ABLE TO MAKE MUSIC YOU WANTED TO. YOU DIDN'T HAVE TO WORRY ABOUT RENTING A PRACTICE SPACE OR FIGURE OUT WHEN ANOTHER BAND WOULD BE IN THERE OR WORRY ABOUT IF YOUR STUFF IS GOING TO GET STOLEN.
-DAVID PAJO

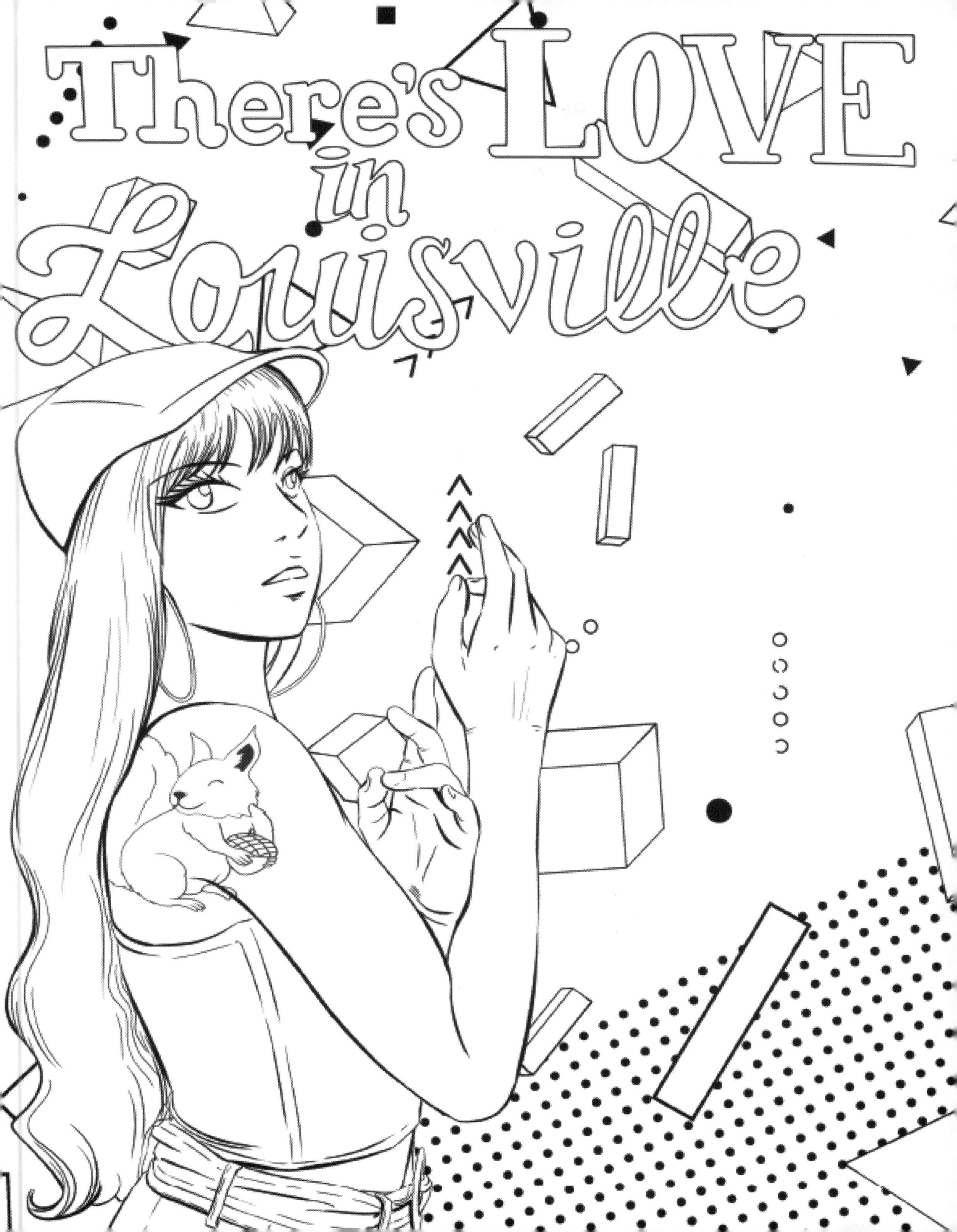
There's LOVE
in
Louisville

HOUNDSMOUTH
-MCKENZIE-

SUPPORT LOCAL!
SUPPORT BLACK!
SUPPORT IMMIGRANTS!
WE ARE WHAT MAKES LOUISVILLE GREAT!

LOUISVILLE FACTS #1

1. Louisville is one of the oldest cities west of Appalachian Mountain range.

2. Louisville is home to the oldest Mississippi-style steamboat in existence. The Belle of Louisville turned 100 years old in 2014!

3. The song "Happy Birthday" was written by two Louisville sisters, Patty and Mildred J. Hill.

4. Louisville's Jefferson Memorial Park is the largest municipal urban forest in the United States. It sits on over 6,000 acres of land!

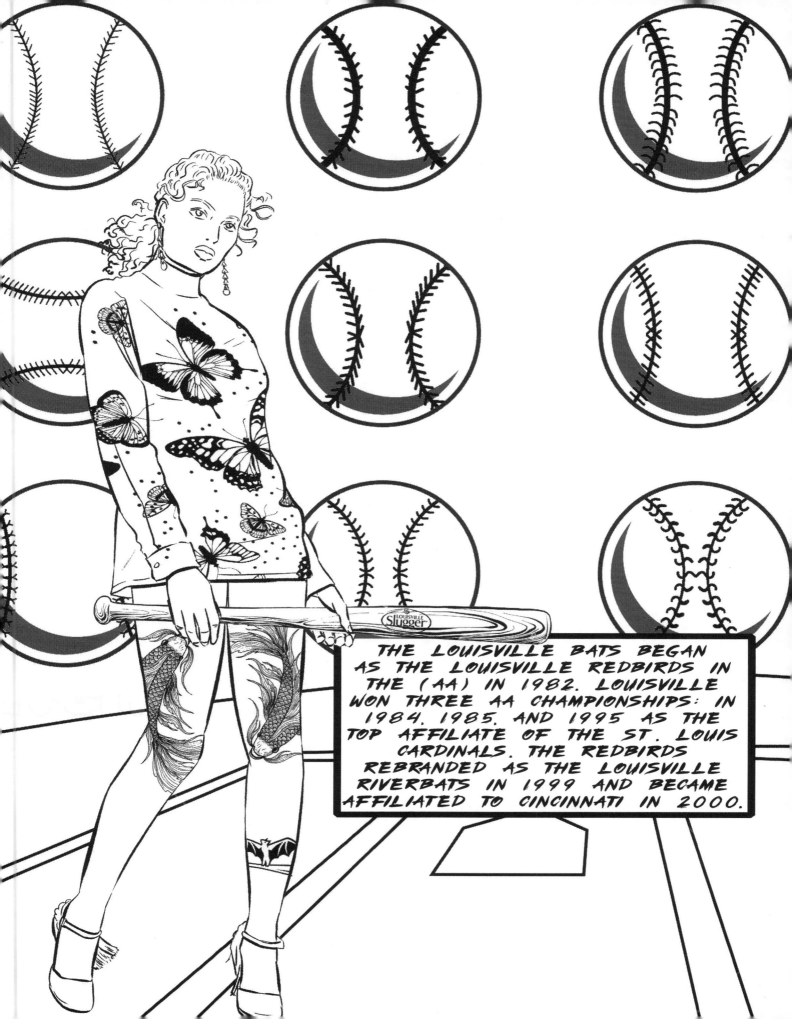

THE LOUISVILLE BATS BEGAN AS THE LOUISVILLE REDBIRDS IN THE (AA) IN 1982. LOUISVILLE WON THREE AA CHAMPIONSHIPS: IN 1984, 1985, AND 1995 AS THE TOP AFFILIATE OF THE ST. LOUIS CARDINALS. THE REDBIRDS REBRANDED AS THE LOUISVILLE RIVERBATS IN 1999 AND BECAME AFFILIATED TO CINCINNATI IN 2000.

TYRANT FT.
KORI BLACK
-TYRANT-

IN LOUISVILLE, AT THE CORNER OF FOURTH AND WALNUT, IN THE CENTER OF THE SHOPPING DISTRICT, I WAS SUDDENLY OVERWHELMED WITH THE REALIZATION THAT I LOVED ALL THOSE PEOPLE, THAT THEY WERE MINE AND I THEIRS, THAT WE COULD NOT BE ALIEN TO ONE ANOTHER EVEN THOUGH WE WERE TOTAL STRANGERS.
-THOMAS MERTON

TASTE OF LOUISVILLE #1
BENEDICTINE SPREAD

Ya'll want something different? Benedictine Spread is where it's at. It's basic. Cucumber and cream cheese. You don't need to be at High Tea to enjoy this spread that originates from Louisville. Jane Benedict, a caterer in Louisville, created this in the 1890's. This can be used as a dip or a spread. This is not as known as some other dishes here in Louisville, but it needs to be. It's on some menus, but make it at home. Blend a package of cream cheese with a seeded cucumber. Add some onion, a little bit of mayonaise, and spread it onto your bread.

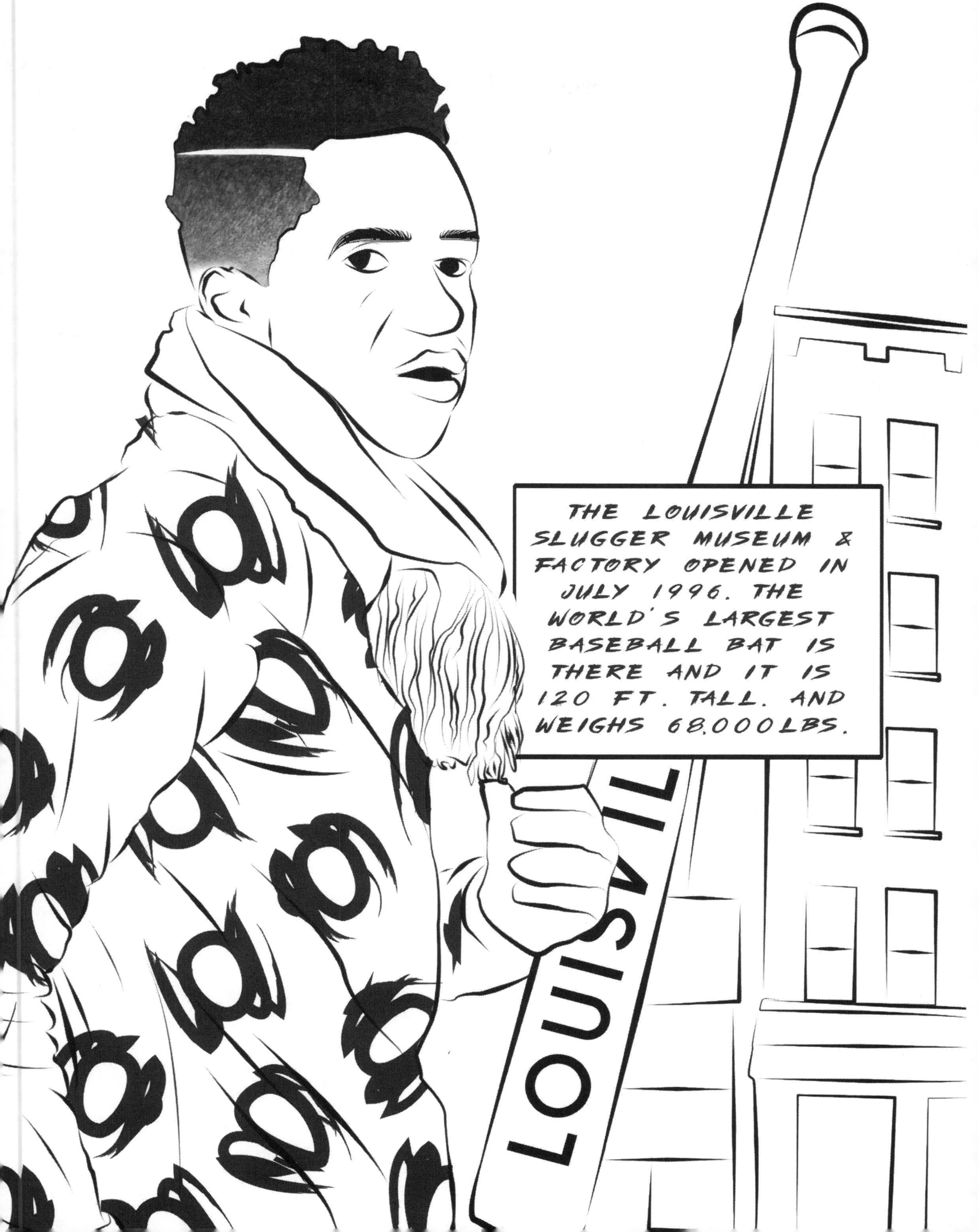
THE LOUISVILLE SLUGGER MUSEUM & FACTORY OPENED IN JULY 1996. THE WORLD'S LARGEST BASEBALL BAT IS THERE AND IT IS 120 FT. TALL. AND WEIGHS 68,000LBS.
LOUISVIL

KIANA AND
THE SUN KINGS
-ANYTHING YOU WANT-

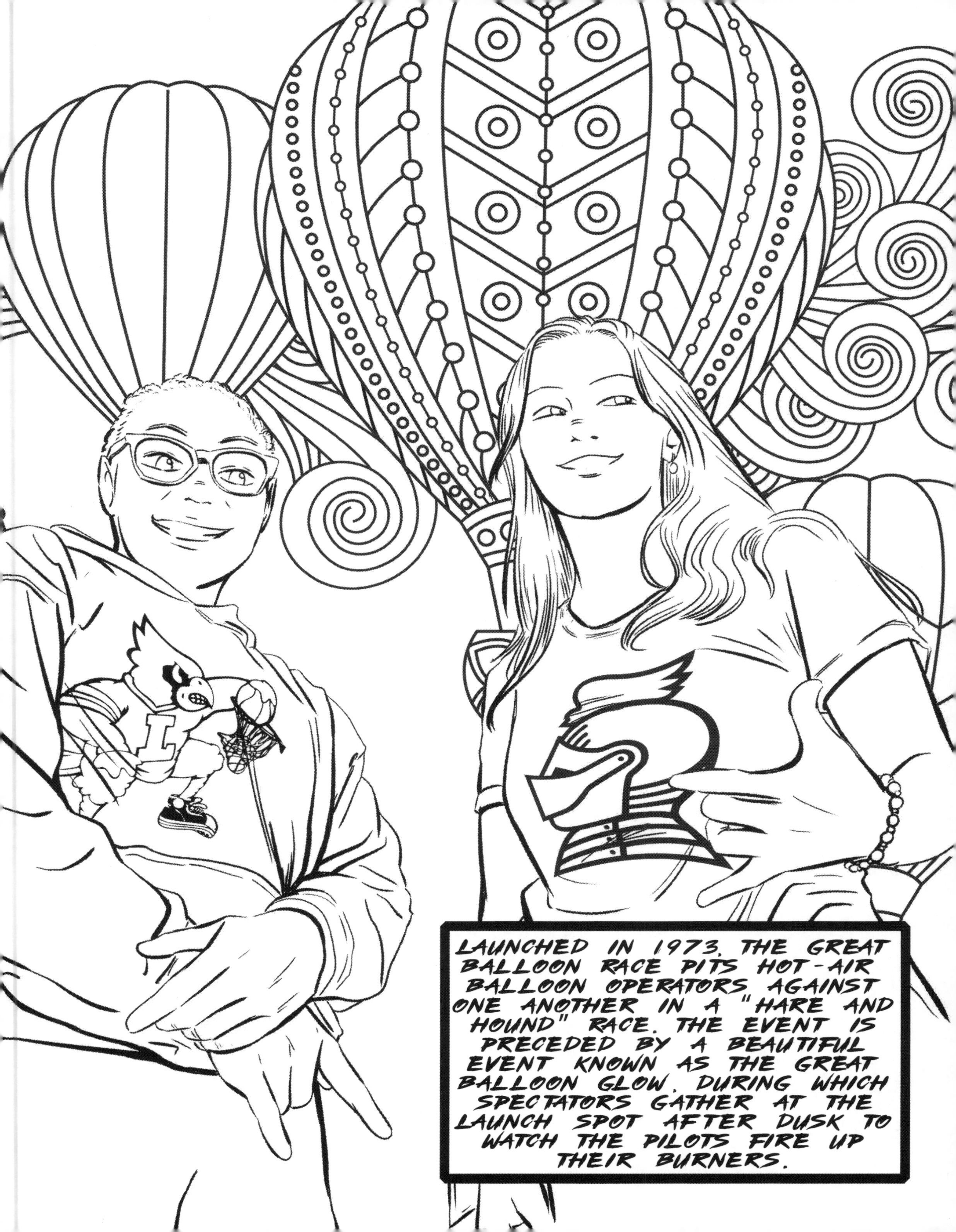
LAUNCHED IN 1973, THE GREAT BALLOON RACE PITS HOT-AIR BALLOON OPERATORS AGAINST ONE ANOTHER IN A "HARE AND HOUND" RACE. THE EVENT IS PRECEDED BY A BEAUTIFUL EVENT KNOWN AS THE GREAT BALLOON GLOW, DURING WHICH SPECTATORS GATHER AT THE LAUNCH SPOT AFTER DUSK TO WATCH THE PILOTS FIRE UP THEIR BURNERS.

THE N8VS
-GOOD DOPE-

LOUISVILLE FACTS #2

1. Ninety-five percent of the world's bourbon is produced in Kentucky. The best way to experience it all is to complete the Kentucky Bourbon Trail, To explore even more, the Trail covers the route from Louisville to Lexington.

2. 90% of the disco balls in the U.S. are produced in Louisville. Most of the mirror balls are made by National Products on Baxter Ave. They'be been in the disco ball business for over 50 years.

3. Louisville is home to the biggest baseball bat in the world. Baseball fans know that Louisville Sluggers are the best bats in the business. At the Slugger Museum in Louisville, you can see a 120-foot tall and 68,000-pound baseball made of steel.

5 FAMOUS MOVIES FILMED IN LOUISVILLE

Goldfinger (1964)
Local filming location: Bowman Field, Fort Knox
The plot of this classic Bond flick centers around a plan to steal from Fort Knox, The Louisville connection is Bowman Field, where the character Pussy Galore's team of female pilots meets with James Bond.

Abby (1974)
Local filming location: Louisville
A Blaxploitation version of the "The Exorcist" where the woman is possessed by an African sex demon. The Direct, William Girdler is from Louisville as well. So.....represent.

Stripes (1981)
Local filming location: Downtown Louisville, River Road, George Rogers Clark Memorial Bridge
You will instanly see Louisville in the first few minutes of this movie. It's kinda surreal seeing Louisville from 40 years ago.

Secretariat (2010)
Local filming location: Churchill Downs, Wagner's Pharmacy
I mean the film is about a Kentucky Derby Horse. Churchill Downs is the obvious place to shoot. Not accurate but good.

Devil's Revenge (2019)
Local filming location: West Broadway, other Louisville locations
William Shatner stars in this horror movie that is filmed in a lot of interesting locations including Jefferson Community and Technical College. Described as "A down-on-his-luck archaeologist returns from a cave expedition that contains a cursed relic that's also a portal to Hell. He discovers that the only way to stop the curse on his family is to go back to the cave and destroy the relic."

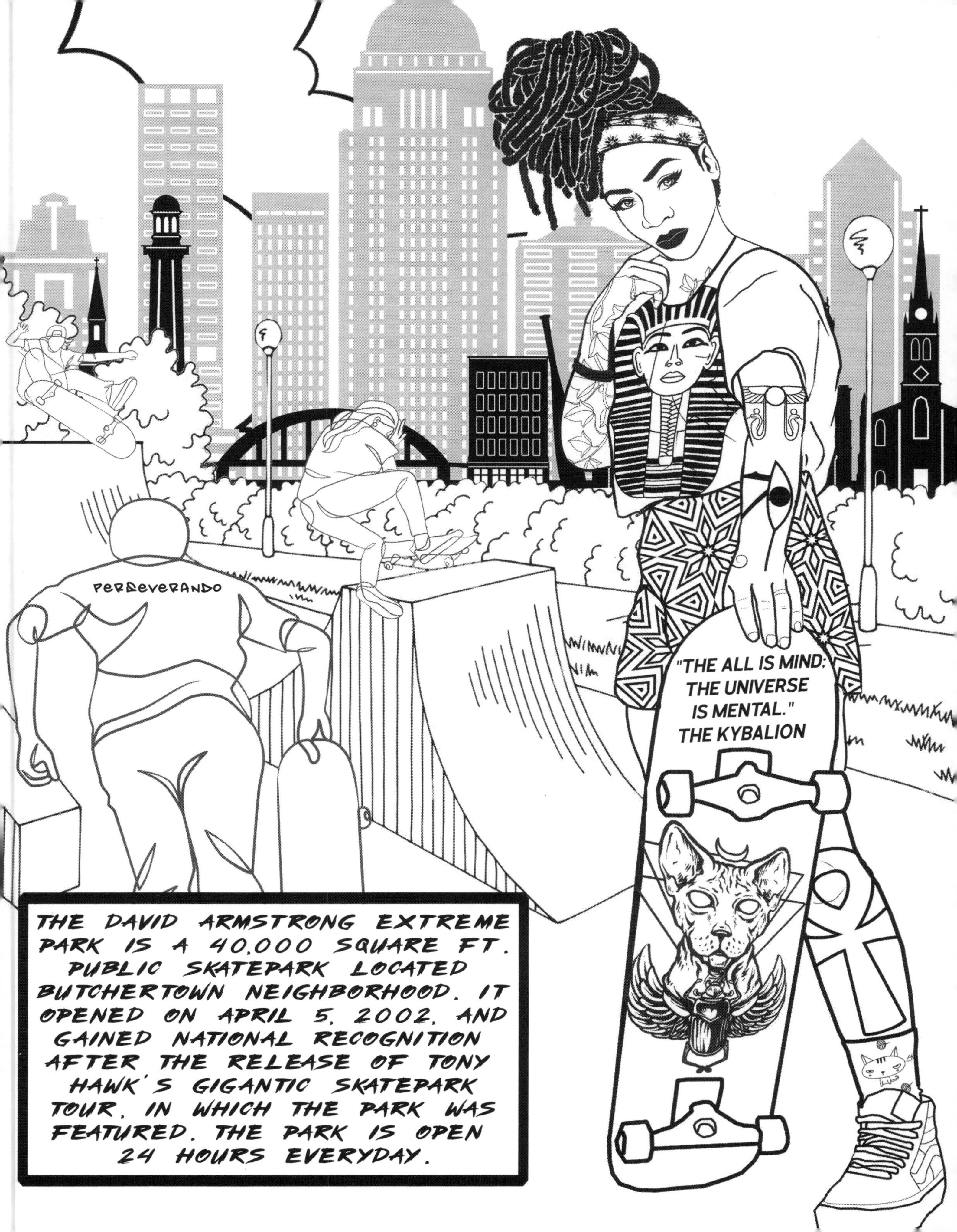
PERSEVERANDO
"THE ALL IS MIND; THE UNIVERSE IS MENTAL." THE KYBALION
THE DAVID ARMSTRONG EXTREME PARK IS A 40,000 SQUARE FT. PUBLIC SKATEPARK LOCATED BUTCHERTOWN NEIGHBORHOOD. IT OPENED ON APRIL 5, 2002, AND GAINED NATIONAL RECOGNITION AFTER THE RELEASE OF TONY HAWK'S GIGANTIC SKATEPARK TOUR, IN WHICH THE PARK WAS FEATURED. THE PARK IS OPEN 24 HOURS EVERYDAY.

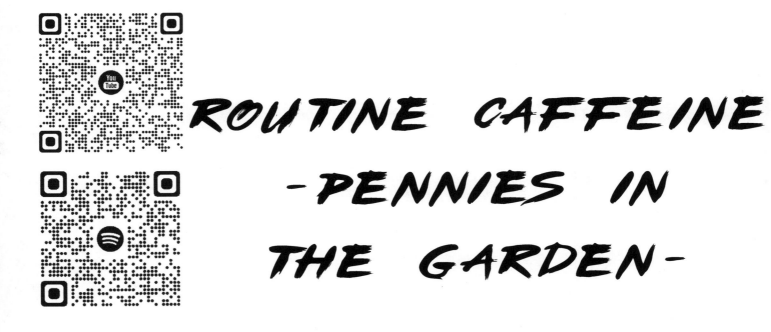

ROUTINE CAFFEINE
-PENNIES IN
THE GARDEN-

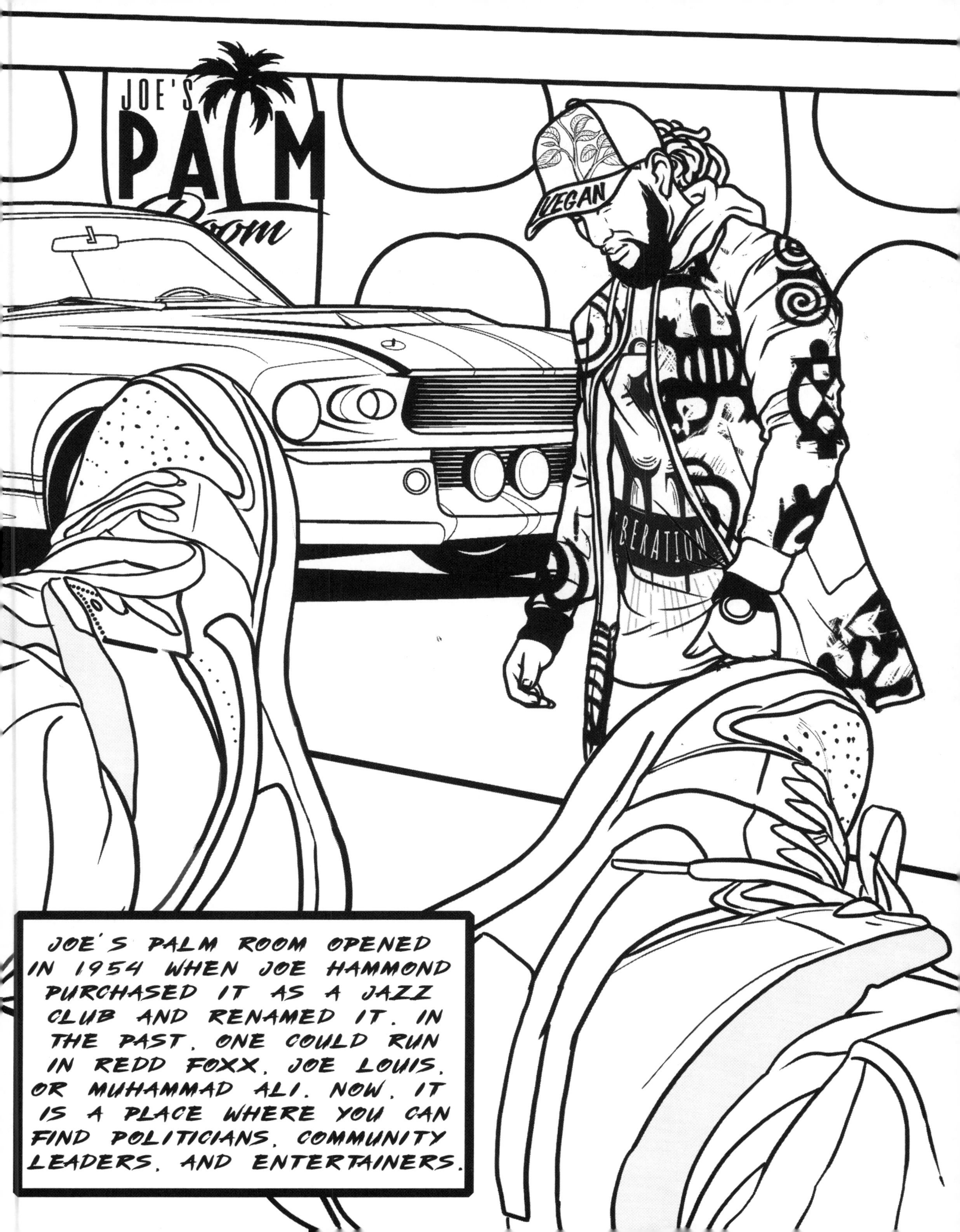
JOE'S PALM Room
VEGAN
JOE'S PALM ROOM OPENED IN 1954 WHEN JOE HAMMOND PURCHASED IT AS A JAZZ CLUB AND RENAMED IT. IN THE PAST, ONE COULD RUN IN REDD FOXX, JOE LOUIS, OR MUHAMMAD ALI. NOW, IT IS A PLACE WHERE YOU CAN FIND POLITICIANS, COMMUNITY LEADERS, AND ENTERTAINERS.

MARZZ
-FEELIN' ME-

LOUISVILLE IS A PLACE WITH NO LA-BELS. IT'S NOT THE SOUTH, IT'S NOT CHICAGO, AND YOU DON'T THINK OF IT AS YOU THINK OF NEW YORK OR LA. IT HAS SOME SOUTHERN ROMANTICISM TO IT, BUT ALSO A NORTHERN PROGRESSIVISM, THIS WEIRD URBAN ISLAND IN THE MIDDLE OF THE STATE OF KENTUCKY THAT HAS ALWAYS PRO-VIDED A FERTILE, OFTEN DARK, BED. FOR US, LOUISVILLE AND THE SURROUNDING AREAS ARE THE CENTER OF MASSIVE CREATIVITY AND MASSIVE WEIRDNESS. THE PLACE HAS ITS FLAWS: YOU MOVE AWAY, BUT YOU'RE ALWAYS GOING TO COME BACK.
-JIM JAMES

TASTE OF LOUISVILLE #2
MINT JULEP

A traditional mint julep is made with just four ingredients: bourbon and simple syrup are mixed with fresh mint and served over crushed ice. What you sip out of matters too. Usually, a traditional silver Julep cup is used. If you can't have that, a Derby glass works.

Here's the thing, though: Louisville can't actually claim the Mint Julep. But it is the official drink of the Kentucky Derby since 1938.

Ingredients
8 mint leaves
1/4 ounce simple syrup
2 ounces bourbon
Garnish: mint sprig
Garnish: Angostura bitters (optional)

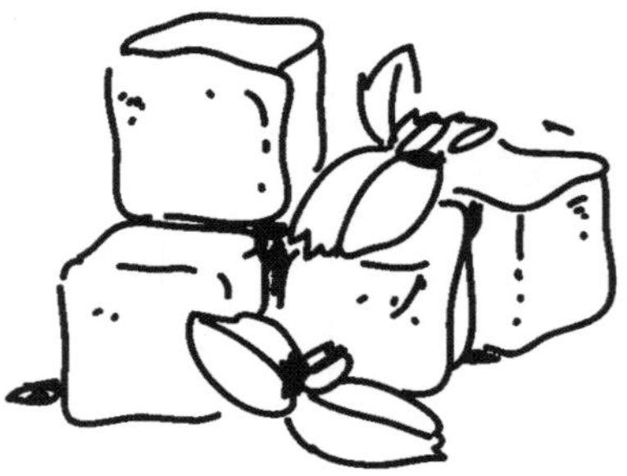

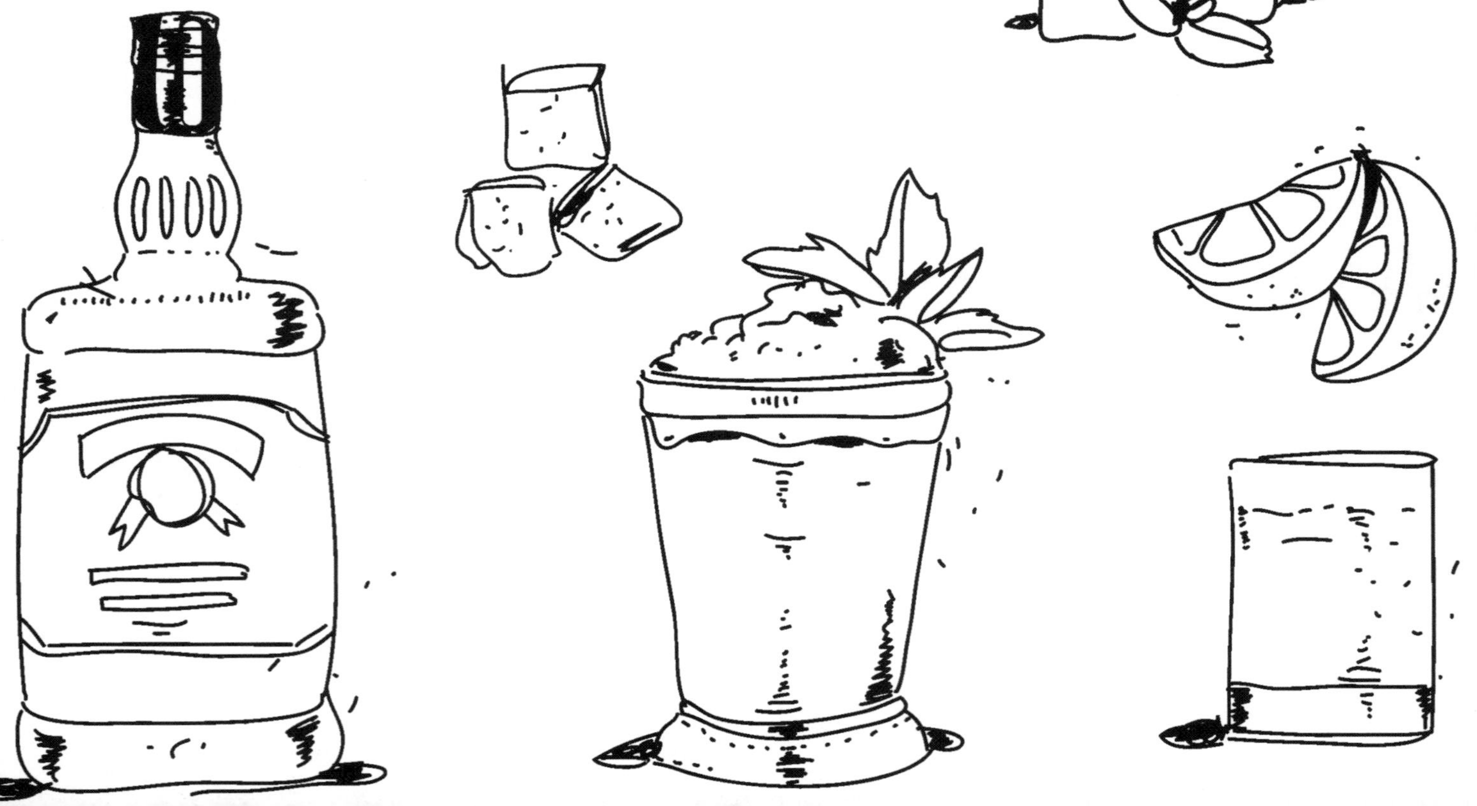

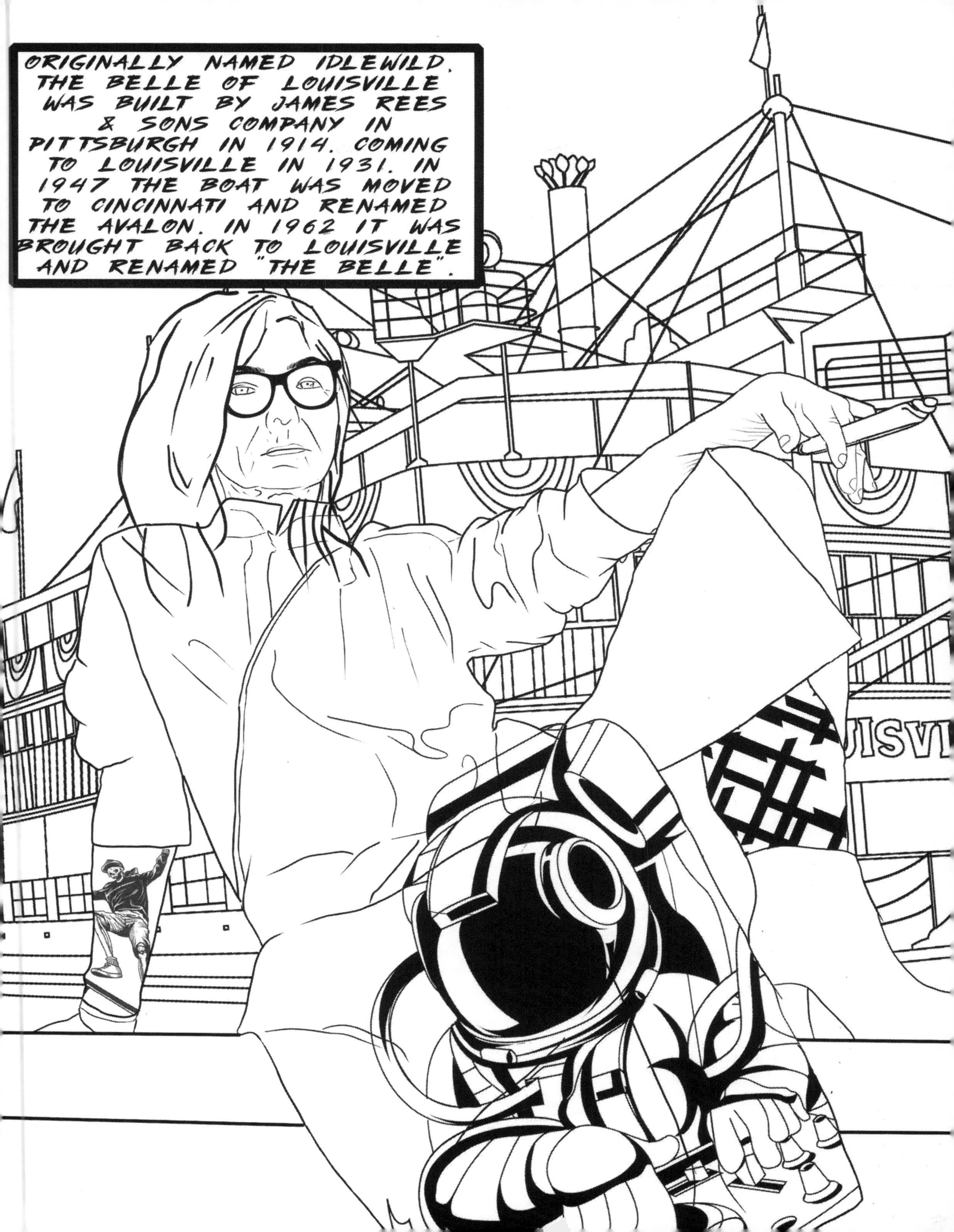
ORIGINALLY NAMED IDLEWILD, THE BELLE OF LOUISVILLE WAS BUILT BY JAMES REES & SONS COMPANY IN PITTSBURGH IN 1914, COMING TO LOUISVILLE IN 1931. IN 1947 THE BOAT WAS MOVED TO CINCINNATI AND RENAMED THE AVALON. IN 1962 IT WAS BROUGHT BACK TO LOUISVILLE AND RENAMED "THE BELLE".
UISVI

YONS
-ROLIO-

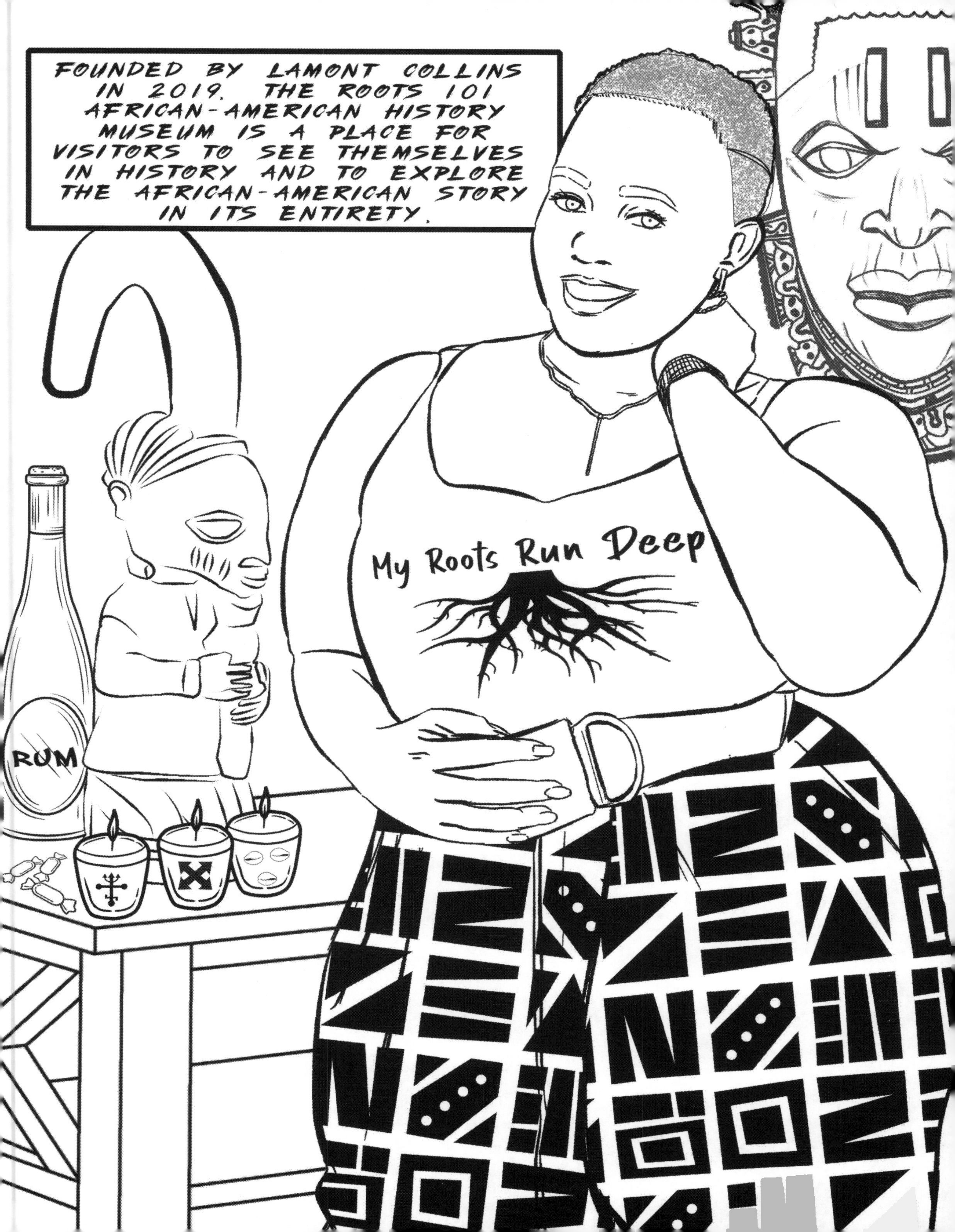
FOUNDED BY LAMONT COLLINS IN 2019, THE ROOTS 101 AFRICAN-AMERICAN HISTORY MUSEUM IS A PLACE FOR VISITORS TO SEE THEMSELVES IN HISTORY AND TO EXPLORE THE AFRICAN-AMERICAN STORY IN ITS ENTIRETY.
My Roots Run Deep
RUM

MY MORNING JACKET

JACKET

-TYRONE-

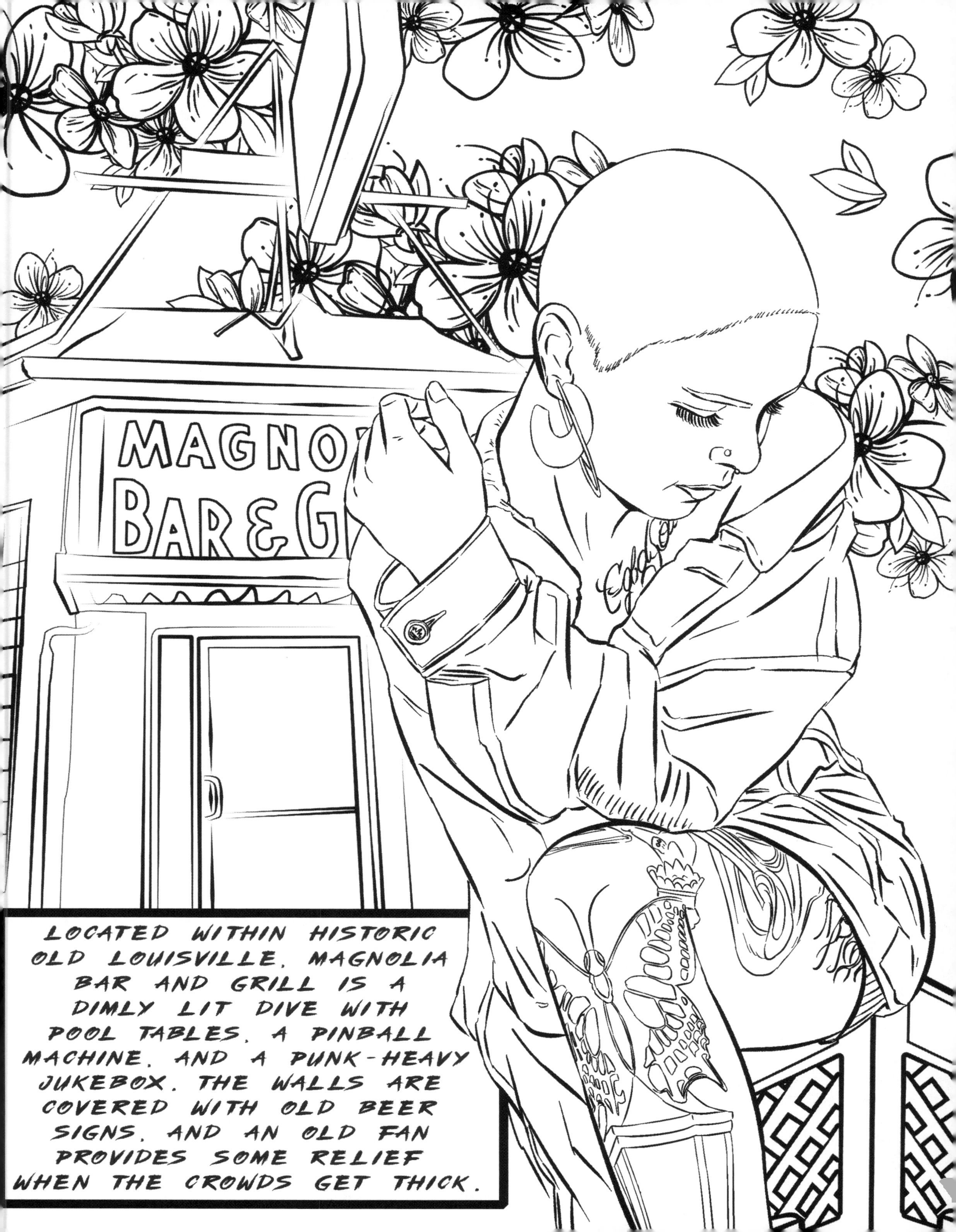
LOCATED WITHIN HISTORIC OLD LOUISVILLE, MAGNOLIA BAR AND GRILL IS A DIMLY LIT DIVE WITH POOL TABLES, A PINBALL MACHINE, AND A PUNK-HEAVY JUKEBOX. THE WALLS ARE COVERED WITH OLD BEER SIGNS, AND AN OLD FAN PROVIDES SOME RELIEF WHEN THE CROWDS GET THICK.

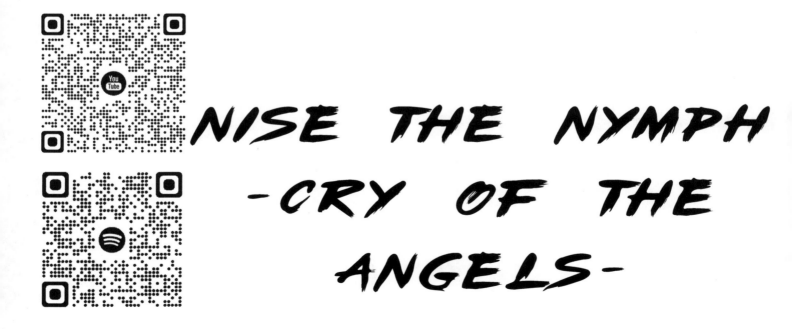

NISE THE NYMPH
-CRY OF THE
ANGELS-

LOUISVILLE FACTS #3

1. Over 100,000 Mint Juleps are served during the Kentucky Derby and Kentucky Oaks.
A classic Mint Julep is served with bourbon and is the official drink of the Kentucky Derby.

2. Tourism is the third-largest revenue-producing industry in Kentucky. Kentucky is known for horses, bourbon, Southern food, Mammoth Cave, and more.

3. Kentucky Derby Winners are covered with 554 roses. 554 roses are used in the garland presented to the winner of the Kentucky Derby. Kentucky Oaks winners are blanketed in lilies, which is why the race holds the nickname Lillies for the Fillies.

5 LOUISVILLE LOCATIONS IN JACK HARLOW SONGS

Song: Walk in the Park
Lyric: "I ain't never rocked no Pacsun. I was off the pack at the mall St. Matt."
Reference: Harlow is referring to Mall St. Matthew's, located in the east part of the city. Address: 5000 Shelbyville Rd.

Song: Route 66
Lyric: "'Cause you left and you not 'round. Need a julep and a hot brown."
Reference: The Hot Brown he's referring to is the official sandwich of the city of Louisville and was invented at the historic Brown hotel in the 1920's.
Address: 335 W. Broadway

Song: Rendezvous
Lyric: "Turkey on ciabatta from the Deli, shout to Morris."
Reference: Morris' Deli is located just outside the Highland's neighborhood and has been around since the 80's.
Address: 2228 Taylorsville Rd.

Song: Baxter Avenue
Reference: The real Baxter Avenue runs through the Highland's neighborhood alongside some of the city's best bars and restaurants.

Song: What's Poppin'
Lyric: "In the 'Ville and I move like a don, Eating fettuccine at Vincenzo's"
Reference: Vincenzo's Italian restaurant is a long time Louisville staple.
Address: 150 S. 5th St.

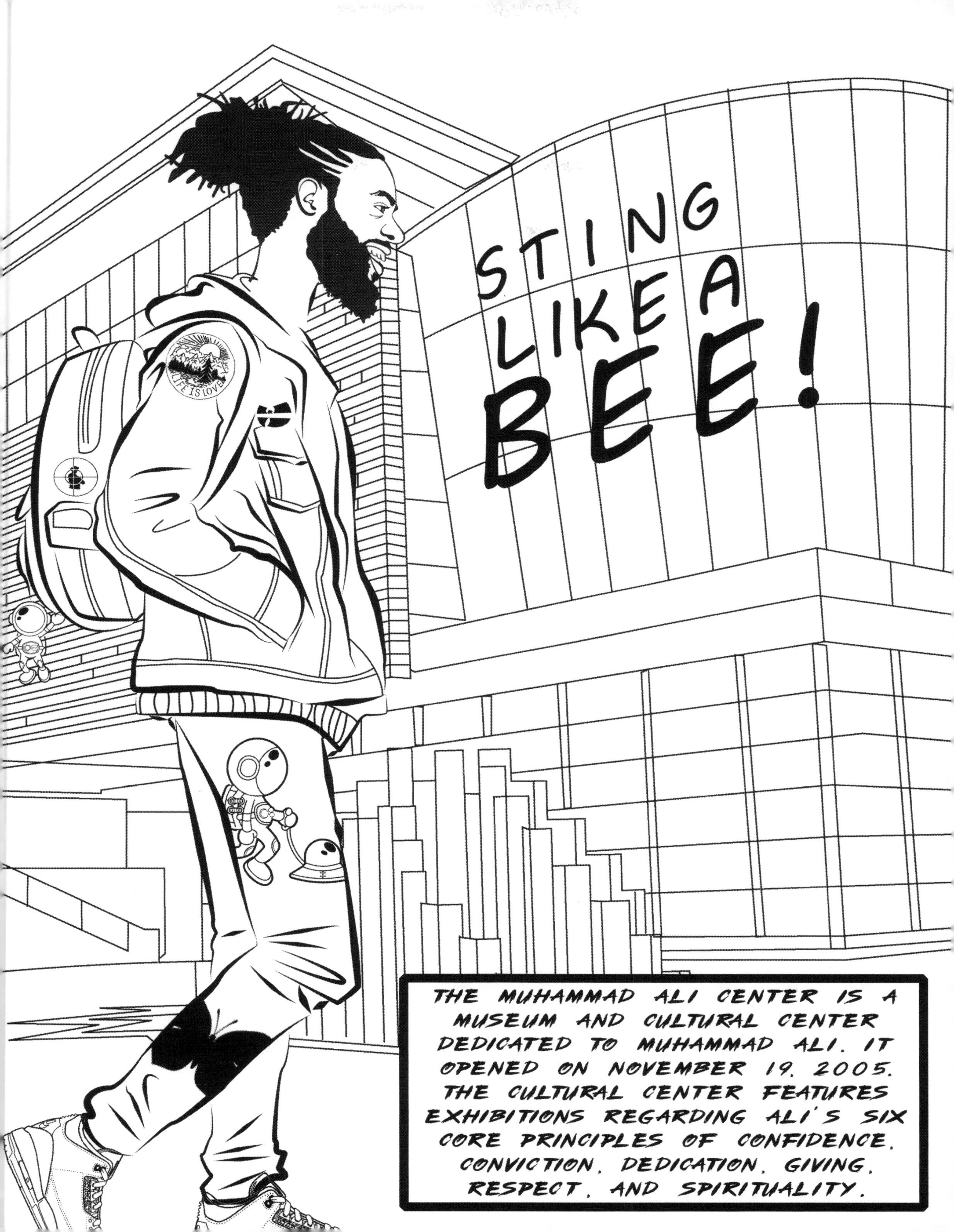
STING LIKE A BEE!
LIFE IS LOVE
THE MUHAMMAD ALI CENTER IS A MUSEUM AND CULTURAL CENTER DEDICATED TO MUHAMMAD ALI. IT OPENED ON NOVEMBER 19, 2005. THE CULTURAL CENTER FEATURES EXHIBITIONS REGARDING ALI'S SIX CORE PRINCIPLES OF CONFIDENCE, CONVICTION, DEDICATION, GIVING, RESPECT, AND SPIRITUALITY.

JORDAN JETSON

-BLESSED-

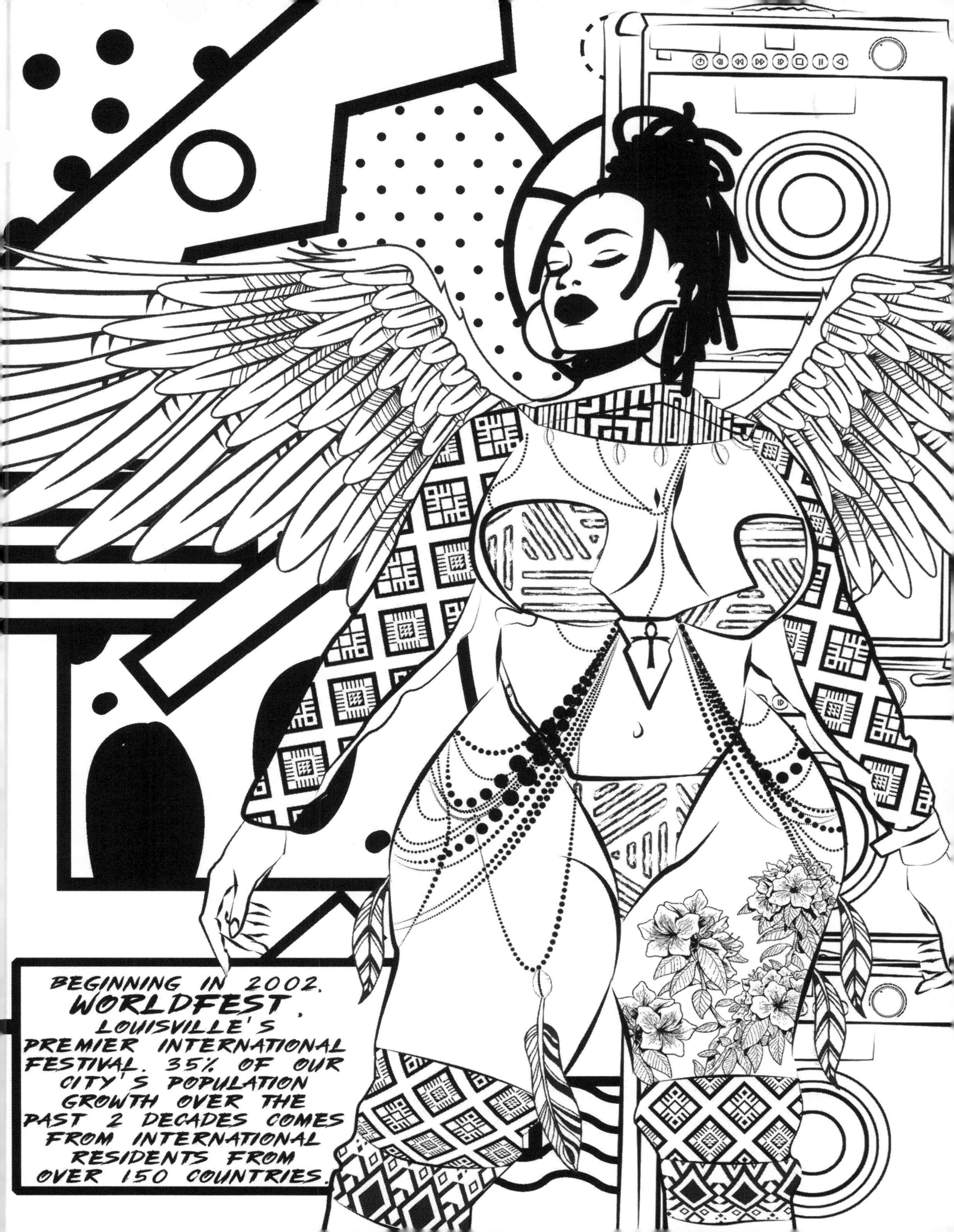
BEGINNING IN 2002, WORLDFEST, LOUISVILLE'S PREMIER INTERNATIONAL FESTIVAL. 35% OF OUR CITY'S POPULATION GROWTH OVER THE PAST 2 DECADES COMES FROM INTERNATIONAL RESIDENTS FROM OVER 150 COUNTRIES.

JACK HARLOW
-BAXTER AVENUE-

LOUISVILLE, AN HOUR AFTER DARK, IS A CARPET OF GILT THUMBTACKS BELOW THEM, WITH STRAIGHT, TWIN-KLING LINES LIKE STRINGS OF BEADS LEADING OUT FROM IT. SOUTHEAST-WARD NOW, TOWARD THE TENNESSEE STATE-LINE. ("JANE BROWN'S BODY")
-CORNELL WOOLRICH

D---Y PIE

Derby Pie™ is my favorite dessert from Louisville. Created by the Kern family in 1954, the traditional version of the pie consists of a layer of walnuts over a layer of chocolate, all in a flaky pie crust. As you can see, Derby Pie™ is trademarked and the inventors don't let anybody use the name on their menu. If you want it, you can find it in the frozen aisle at the grocery. That being said, you can find freshly baked knockoffs all over Louisville. Don't get it twisted, whether it is called a Chocolate Pecan Pie or anything else, it is amazing. Get you some today or make your own.

Ingredients

- 1 (9 inch) pie crust pastry
- 1 cup light corn syrup
- 1 cup white sugar
- 4 eggs
- 1¼ cups chocolate chips
- 1 cup chopped pecans
- ½ cup butter, melted
- 2 tablespoons bourbon
  (Optional)
- 1 teaspoon vanilla extract

Directions

Step 1
Preheat oven to 350 degrees F (175 degrees C). Press pie crust into a 9-inch pie plate.

Step 2
Beat corn syrup, white sugar, and eggs together in a bowl using an electric mixer on low speed until well blended;

stir in chocolate chips, pecans, butter, bourbon, and vanilla extract. Pour mixture into the prepared pie crust.

Step 3
Bake in the preheated oven until set, 45 to 50 minutes.

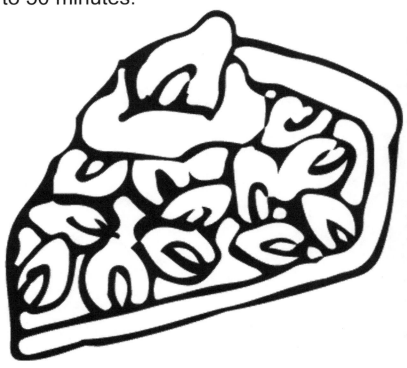

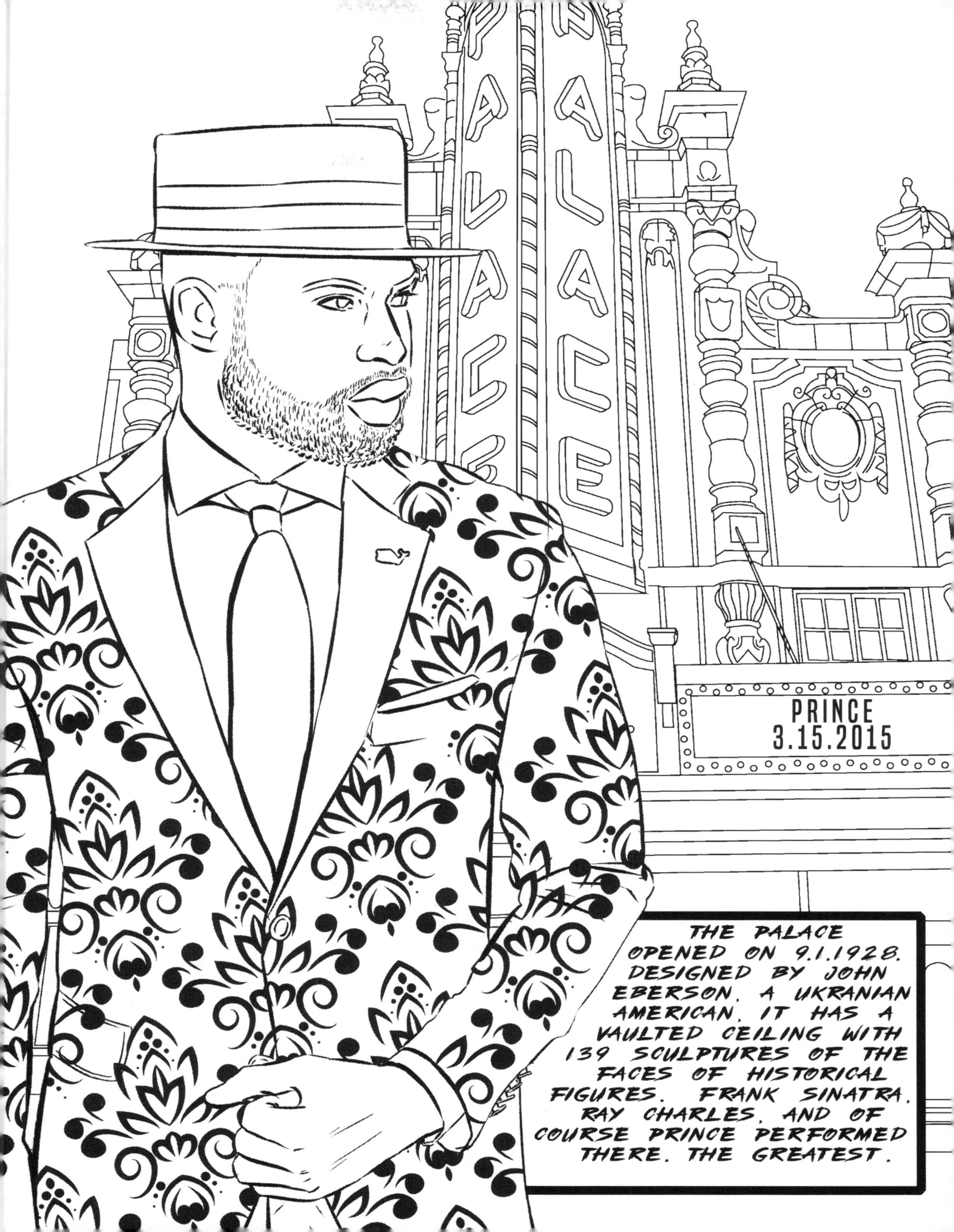
PALACE
PRINCE
3.15.2015
THE PALACE OPENED ON 9.1.1928. DESIGNED BY JOHN EBERSON, A UKRANIAN AMERICAN, IT HAS A VAULTED CEILING WITH 139 SCULPTURES OF THE FACES OF HISTORICAL FIGURES. FRANK SINATRA, RAY CHARLES, AND OF COURSE PRINCE PERFORMED THERE. THE GREATEST.

KASANOVA
-KY STATE OF
MIND-

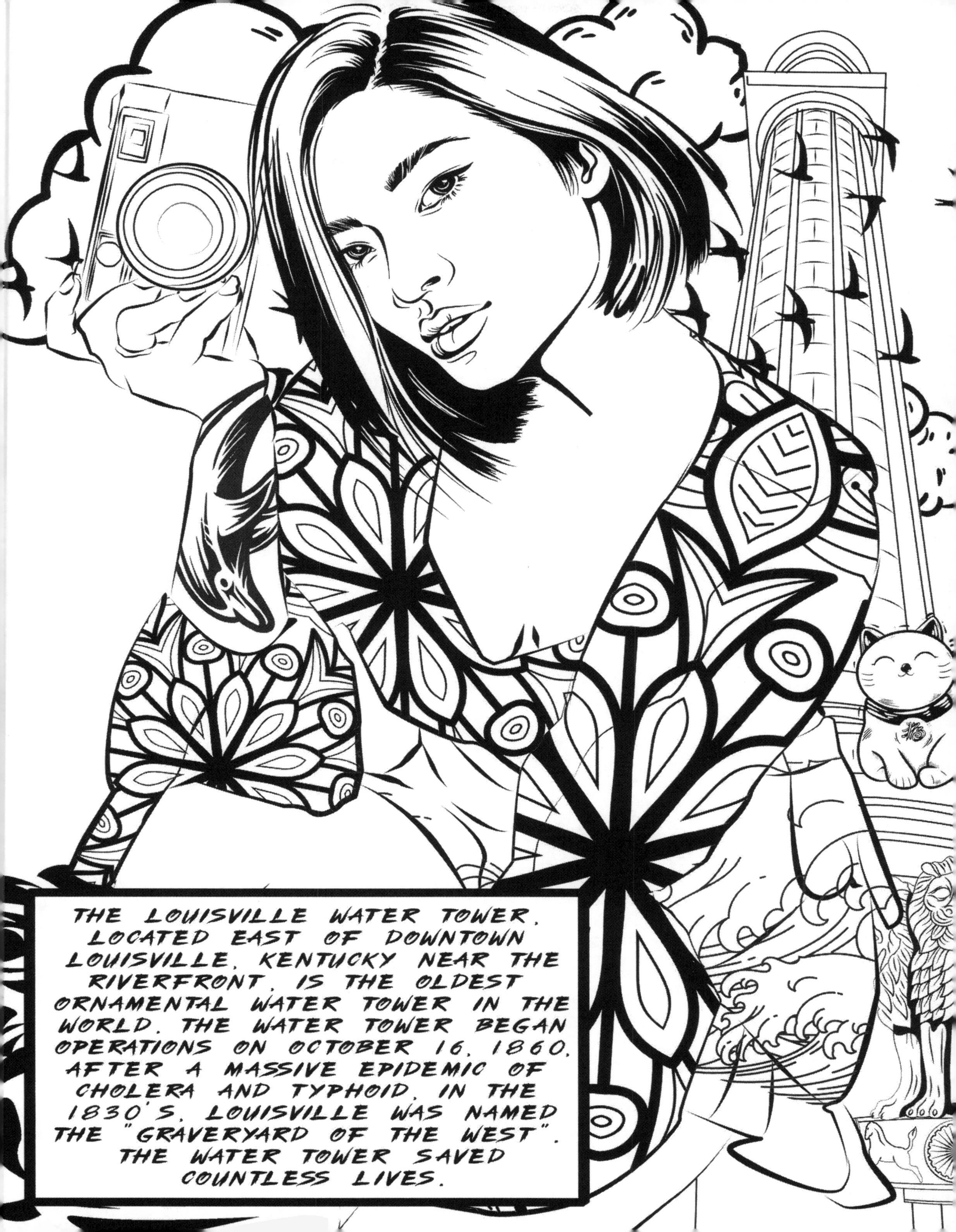
THE LOUISVILLE WATER TOWER, LOCATED EAST OF DOWNTOWN LOUISVILLE, KENTUCKY NEAR THE RIVERFRONT, IS THE OLDEST ORNAMENTAL WATER TOWER IN THE WORLD. THE WATER TOWER BEGAN OPERATIONS ON OCTOBER 16, 1860, AFTER A MASSIVE EPIDEMIC OF CHOLERA AND TYPHOID. IN THE 1830'S, LOUISVILLE WAS NAMED THE "GRAVERYARD OF THE WEST". THE WATER TOWER SAVED COUNTLESS LIVES.

THE REAL YOUNG
PRODIGYS
-JUSTICE 4 ALL-

LOUISVILLE FACTS #4

1. The first successful hand transplant in history was performed at the Kleinert Kutz Hand Care Center in 1999.

2. Louisville's famous Seelbach Hotel served as the inspiration for F. Scott Fitzgerald's novel "The Great Gatsby." Several other elements of the city are included in this bestseller as well.

3. The Kentucky State Fair, held every August at the Kentucky Fair and Expo Center, is the largest air-conditioned state fair in the country.

4. The first library that allowed African Americans as patrons was built in Louisville in 1908.

Louisville has a long musical tradtion that is often overlooked. This crossword puzzle is full of musicians that made it big from our city. Find them. Enjoy them.

(This list is far from complete. It's only a drop in the bucket.)

```
F M H A E P M V K J W L A M E L L E H A R R I S A J E Q O Q
D B H R J Z X Z I O Q A E Q B Z Y W X K B A P Z X X W T V S
N L S Q Q T R Y T M O H K D K Y F Y K F S N J Z J F H R X E
T K E E N R O B S O N A O J U R E D A V I D G R I S S O M N
M K M F N Y R B A M Q F P Y X L V D Y I S O U K B I X M K O
S X A K L D E A T L B O Q F M C L A D G V J B V V V O Q H J
D V J C Y K P B E O F L A W E W I G H O W S K E S V F K U E
X T M N B Y M I B F G W T A K G O I R U A Q S U R A E W X V
Z H I F M M E S R G F N J C Y R N Y R K A T Y X E W V T T O
L N J Z K Q W N O Y I E C H N A E M E S G J Q S V G U T I L
O T L Z E L Y P S U M I T R A Q L T W E U W E H A R A K D P
W E R A A M S L H Y Y P A I C O H P E T E X C S R B Z J W I
F K Q A F H B V V T K T K S H N A T D O M Y N T T R C V N H
U C G L W N J Q N S M N R H Q Z M X C L L M V A Y Y G T K G
I A K C O E G H W X A G J A H A P O Z D G N L T R S M S R B
K J M A L D T W G A H K W R Z E T O Z R I B H I A O U P F Y
A G E S E A N S V R D M H D J H O X F M N X E C M N N D M L
X N A E A U V A D W X X W W U C N Q Z A L E O M W T E U O N
Z I D Y B U B I P D O B F I G K C I E H S E B A Q I H U D V
Y N E O Y J O C V P E L J C M G Z T O D J O U J A L C C H A
Y R L C S B O R Q E Y R R K E O O N S L P W L O O L X J K E
M O U H V H I Q Z U R R S A J H F G R O X K I R Q E I M T G
M M X X L X P L U B S O L H E M O V M S L B T J R V D Z M
I Y L S N L S N I A H S S O P K L J M A B E X L B W Q H P X
A M E W K J Q L A Y Z I W A T G C Y Q I U K S Z M X A D R G
R N W D M G J F P X M I M A R S H A L L A L L E N A N J I F
M B I T E A A Q N U D F U N W G K T J L X B G R Z D S N N Q
C C S U S I D G R I F F I N Q U W U K I N P H B R G U V B X
Y R N C Z I O S B F W H Y I S U W E D W D X S G W F X Q G D
I G L T V N K V P H O H P A M E R H N Q Z V V I P F Z N O R
```

My Morning Jacket
Jim James
Bryson Tiller
Playa
Nappy Roots
William Oldham
VHS or Beta
Mary Travers
Marshall Allen
NewGrassRevival

Flaw
Love Jones
Joan Osborne
Al Casey
EST GEE
Emperor X
Sid Griffin
David Grissom
Lionel Hampton
Chris Hardwick

Jack Harlow
Lamelle Harris
Meade Lux Lewis
Artimus Pyle
Static Major
Redd Stewart
Hattie Bishop Speed
Vory
Nicole Scherzinger

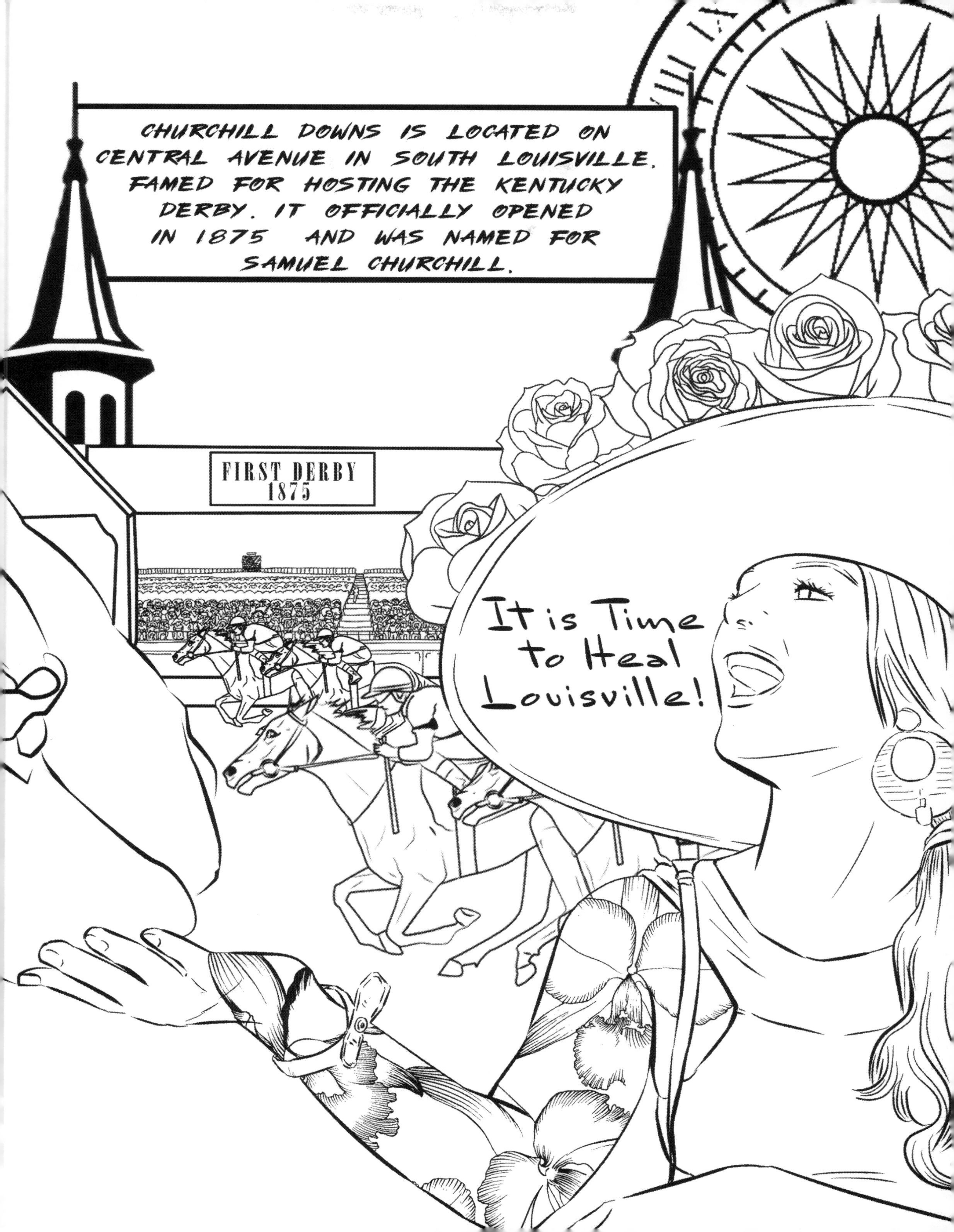
CHURCHILL DOWNS IS LOCATED ON CENTRAL AVENUE IN SOUTH LOUISVILLE. FAMED FOR HOSTING THE KENTUCKY DERBY. IT OFFICIALLY OPENED IN 1875 AND WAS NAMED FOR SAMUEL CHURCHILL.
FIRST DERBY 1875
It is Time to Heal Louisville!

THE JESSE LEES

- SATURDAY -

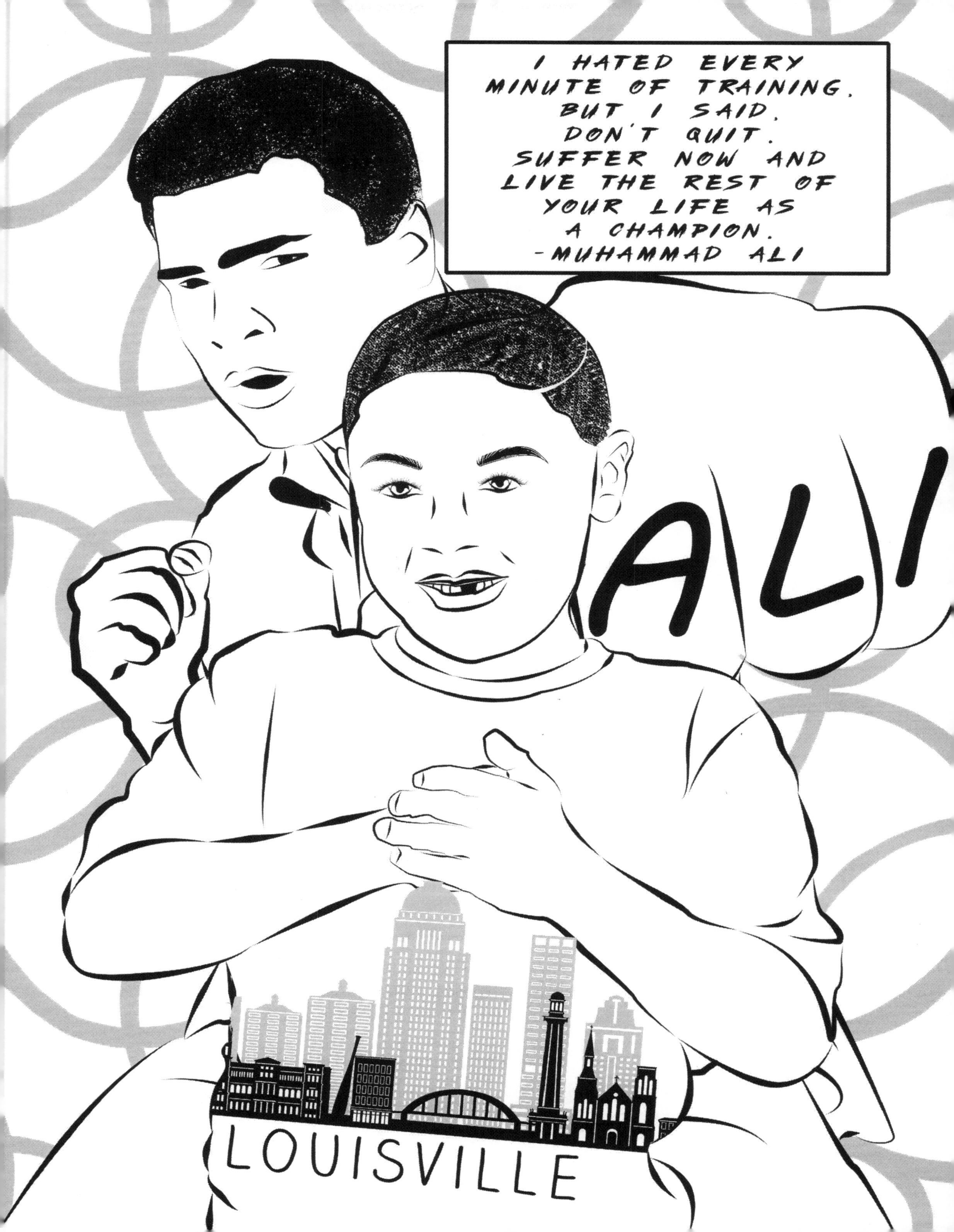
I HATED EVERY MINUTE OF TRAINING. BUT I SAID. DON'T QUIT. SUFFER NOW AND LIVE THE REST OF YOUR LIFE AS A CHAMPION. -MUHAMMAD ALI
ALI
LOUISVILLE

TASTE OF LOUISVILLE #4
THE OLD FASHIONED

The Old Fashioned is Louisville's official cocktail. It's Simple. It's Classic. It's Louisville. Made with bourban, simple syrup, bitters (Angostura), a flamed orange peed, and a cherry garnish. Serve this on the rocks with one of those lowball glasses. Always a winner.

The Old Fashioned was invented in Louisville at the Pendennis Club. A bartender named Tom Bullock created the Old Fashioned in honor of Colonel James E. Pepper. Bullock was an African-American bartender and the first known Black author to publish a cocktail menu. Pepper was a prominent distiller who took the drink to the Waldorf-Astoria Hotel in New York City. New Yorkers disagree with this, but what do they know? They are from New York City.

OLD FASHIONED RECIPE
Ingredients
1/2 teaspoon sugar
3 dashes Angostura bitters
1 teaspoon water
2 ounces bourbon
Garnish: orange peel

Steps
1. Add the sugar and bitters to a rocks glass, then add the water, and stir until the sugar is nearly dissolved.

2. Fill the glass with large ice cubes, add the bourbon, and gently stir to combine.

3. Express the oil of an orange peel over the glass, then drop in.

"I'M RECOGNIZED ALL OVER THE WORLD NOW, BUT MY GREATNESS CAME AND STARTED IN LOUISVILLE, KENTUCKY," ALI SAID IN 1974 AFTER HE DEFEATED GEORGE FOREMAN IN THE FIGHT KNOWN AS THE RUMBLE IN THE JUNGLE. "AND IT'S ONE OF THE GREATEST CITIES IN AMERICA, LOU-ISVILLE, KENTUCKY. AND I PREDICT THAT LOUISVILLE, KENTUCKY WILL HAVE ANOTHER WORLD CHAMPION BECAUSE LOUISVILLE IS THE GREATEST."
-MUHAMMAD ALI

So much has happened in this city over the past few years. Covid shook our country up, and the efforts for reform and change shook our city up. And yet, we Louisvillians still manage to keep smiling. Since coming to this city, the one thing I have realized is that Louisville is its own best-kept secret. Why do I say this? People from different parts of the United States easily recognize how unique this place is. Maybe it was the 4 am bar time or that it's a city that is more aligned to Nashville, Memphis, and New Orleans than other cities closer to it.

Maybe it is the immigrant population that is here.
53,120 foreign-born residents
7.2% share of the total population
1,710 foreign-born entrepreneurs
"Between 2017-2018, Louisville/Jefferson County would have lost around 2,026 people if it weren't for the international migration that settles in the city every year."

Maybe it is because of the natural beauty that surrounds this city.
Maybe it's simply the people, the food, the culture, the mix, the smiles, the peace that makes up Louisville. It's everything and more. If anything happens, let us no longer allow Louisville to be its own best-kept secret.

R.I.P

Breonna Taylor and David McAtee

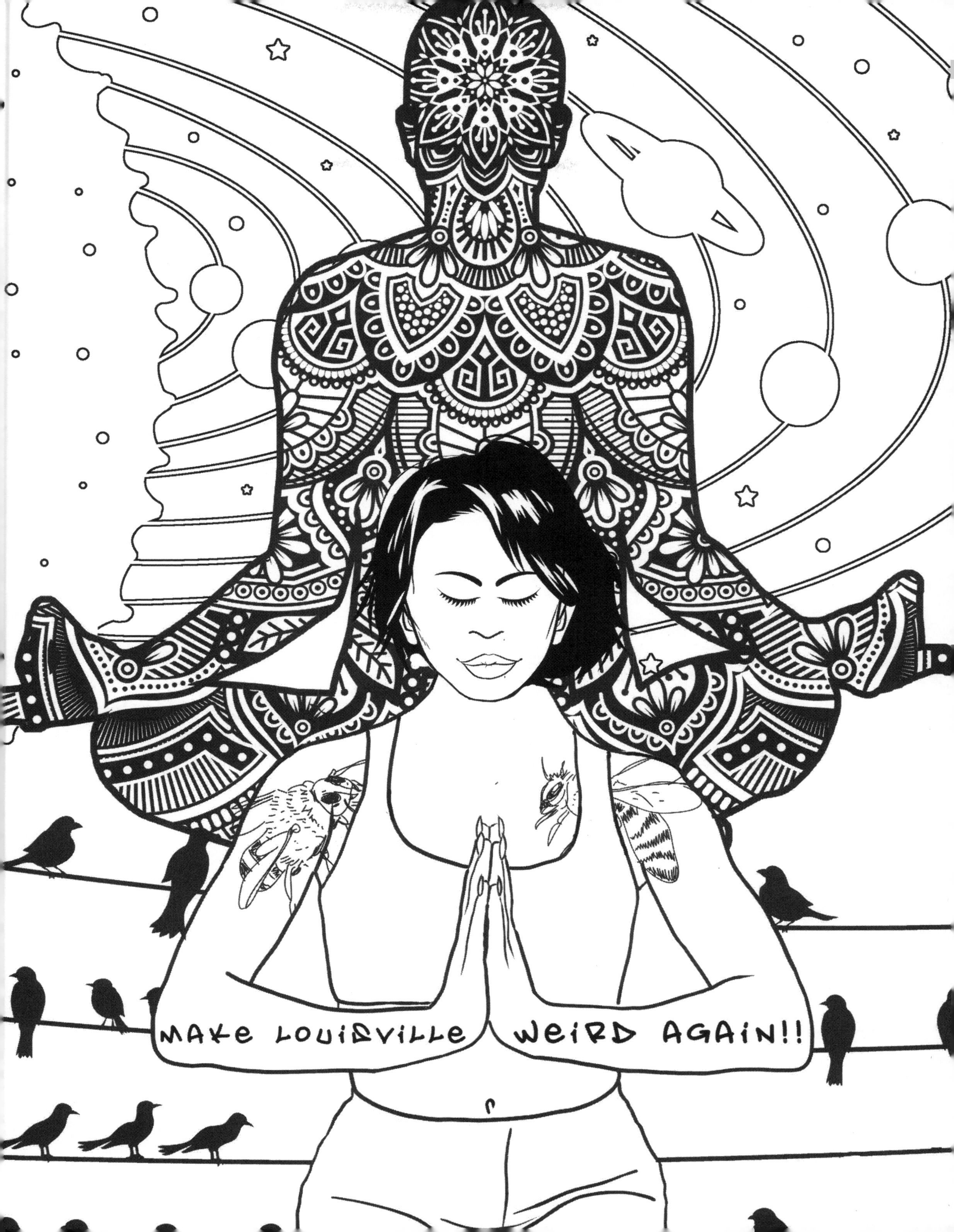
MAKE LOUISVILLE WEIRD AGAIN!!

ELLA FITZGERALD
-LOUISVILLE K.Y.-

LOVE AND LOU

First of all, thank you for purchasing this book. We have worked hard to create a beautiful, custom experience that shows the greatness of my city. This is not your typical coloring or activity book. This book includes coloring pages, wordfinds, fact, recipes, and some of my favorite places in Louisville.

Have fun with this book. Enjoy yourself. Take time to explore this great city of Loisville and realize that this book is just a taste. Stay Connected, Follow us on Instagram @InFlyWeTrustInc, and Stay Fly.

If you like this,
PLEASE, PLEASE, PLEASE
leave a review and find more of our products at

www.InFlyWeTrust.com

-Jide Fresh

The "Love and Lou" Playlist can be found at this link.

Linktr.ee/inflywetrust

Made in United States
Orlando, FL
17 May 2022